P9-ECP-048

DO NOT REMOVE
CARDS FROM POCKET

Few of us see a computer at work, though they help us in all sorts of ways. Clinics, shops, buses and many of the things we use every day are helped by computers, while behind the scenes they make life easier for the police, airlines, banks, engineers and businesses.

Computers are the useful tools of mankind, completing at lightning speed jobs that would take us weeks or months to do. Always people are in control; computers do not "think for themselves" and if they make mistakes it is because people have set up the job wrongly.

One of the most startling achievements of computer technology was the Apollo programme of the USA. Without the computers on the ground, the rockets would never have reached the moon.

Other books in this series

Science versus Crime William Breckon
Man-made Fibres Mike Lyth
Lasers William Burroughs
Man's Future in Space Patrick Moore
The Weather Frank Dalton
The Quest for Fuel John A G Thomas
Spare Parts for People B J Williams

Science in Action

LIVING WITH COMPUTERS

Barry Blakeley

and

Robert Lewis

ISBN 0 85078 214 7

Copyright © 1978 Wayland Publishers Limited
First published in 1978 by
Wayland Publishers Limited, 49 Lansdowne Place,
Hove, East Sussex BN3 1HF

Photoset by Granada Graphics Ltd and
printed in England by Butler and Tanner Ltd,
Frome and London

Contents

2085404

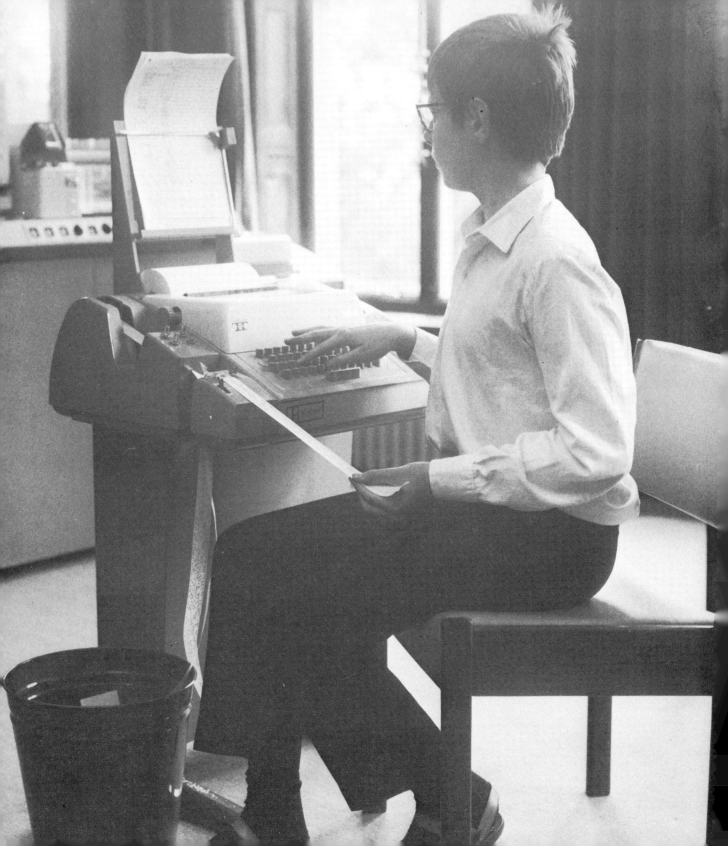

What they are and what they do

Everyone has heard about computers, and most of us have come into contact with them in one way or another. The stocks of food we see in the super-market are usually controlled by com-puter; the roads we travel along have been built with the aid of a computer; the cars we ride in have been partly designed by computer; airline or ferry reservations are recorded on a com-puter, and all the money that goes into and out of bank accounts is checked by computers.

Although a computer plays an impor-tant part in these activities, none of them would be possible without the

A schoolboy learns to use a computer. More and more schools are using computers and training students to work with them.

actions of human beings. The kind of computers we find 'thinking for themselves' in books and on television are really very fictional. Before a computer can help us by doing complicated sums or storing and then looking up pieces of information, they have to be given detailed instructions on what to do. This sounds as if it might be quite easy, but we have all heard stories about computers 'getting it wrong'; this really means that the human operators and programmers have themselves made the mistakes.

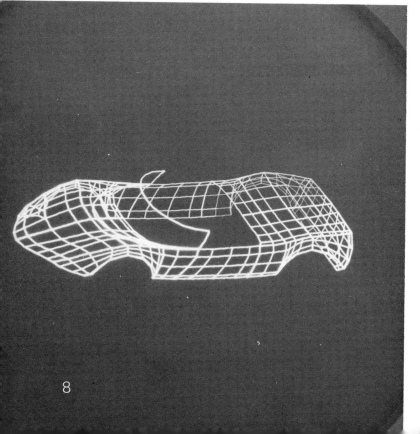

Who are these 'operators' and 'programmers' and what do they have to do? We have said that we have to give the computer detailed instructions of what to do; this job is done by a *programmer* who writes what we call a computer *program.* (Note that we spell the word program — when it means instructions for a computer — in the American way.) Before the programmer can start his job he has to understand exactly what the computer has to do; often he (or she) is helped by a person

Above *Computers help us every day. They keep the airlines running.*

Left *Computers record the money that goes in and out of banks.*

Far Left *Design for cars are often computer-aided. This is a computer design for the body of a sports car.*

Right *Here is just one of the many terminals linked to a giant processing computer. The terminals are spread over a vast area from Switzerland to the north of England.*

known as an *analyst.* The analyst has to work out the whole operation, including those jobs which have to be done by humans. This is a most important part of getting the computer to do useful things. If too many difficult things are left to humans and they make mistakes, the whole operation will be a waste of time and money. There is a saying among computer people, 'Garbage in, garbage out'; in other words, if you put nonsense into the computer, nonsense will come out.

Right *Computer operators at work. Two input devices can be seen. There is a keyboard and also a pile of punched cards.*

Below *The computer has received the imput data and processed it. The output device in this case is a printer. The computer prints the information on a roll of paper for the operator to read off.*

So the analysis of the whole task must be done carefully and then the programmer can write out the instructions (the program) that will ensure the task is done accurately. Here again there may be problems, as the program must be able to take care of the most unusual, though accurate, information. You have probably heard of the gas company computer that sent a bill and then repeated threatening demands for £0.00; that was not the computer's fault.

Let us assume that the work of the analyst and programmer has been done well. The program is stored away in the computer memory and the *operator* instructs the computer to act

upon the instruction. Almost certainly, the program will need some information or *data*. This data may be provided in one of a number of different ways. It may be numbers or names collected from forms and punched onto computer cards. (This is likely to be the way the program itself was fed into the computer.) This data will be processed and the resulting data printed out, as, for example, electricity bills or bank statements. But there are

Above *An early electric card-punching machine.*

Below *A punched card.*

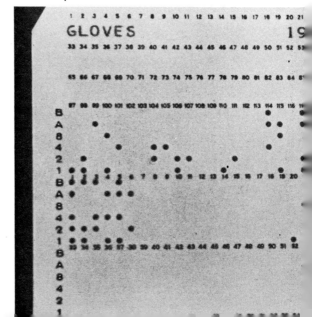

Above *This operator has a keyboard and a video terminal.*

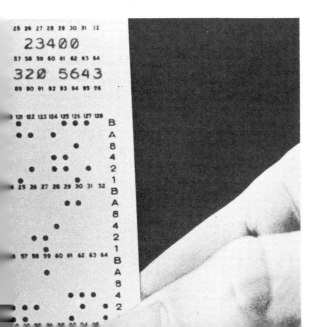

other ways in which the data could be fed into the computer. If you are booking a seat on an aircraft, the booking clerk will type the data on a keyboard (like a typewriter keyboard) and the output from the computer may appear as information on a television screen. For many computer jobs nowadays, the data is collected automatically. Human beings could not count the number of vehicles on a road quickly enough to allow the computer to control the traffic-lights. In this case wires set into the road measure the traffic flow, and the data is fed automatically to the computer. The output from that kind of program is not printed information either; the output is the electrical signals which control the traffic-lights.

Earlier, we mentioned the computer's 'memory'. This is a crucial part, as the computer must be able to accept instructions and store these away so that they can be used time and time again. There are a number of kinds of

Below *A busy computer room. There are three terminals with keyboards and printers, and you can see magnetic tape reels which store data.*

computer memory. Which store is used depends upon how often and how quickly data is needed. It is rather like the way people 'store' telephone numbers. Some numbers are used often and we remember them — they are 'stored' in the brain. Others which are not used so often are written in a diary. Those used occasionally but which we may need, for example a local taxi service, are stored in a telephone directory, and others rarely needed, for example a taxi service in Paris, can be obtained by asking Directory Enquiries. As we go from one level of storage to another, so the amount of data increases, and it takes longer to find. In a computer system, storage is similar. The program being used at the moment is in the computer's memory, often called the 'immediate access' store. Other data is stored on *magnetic discs,* and great amounts of data are stored on *magnetic tape.* All the forms

Left *This magnetic disc drum contains up to 30 million characters of information.*

Left *Magnetic tape is used to store large amounts of data. Tape is kept in racks all carefully labelled.*

Below *Testing a central processing unit. This is the 'brain' of the computer. As you can see, it is a very complicated piece of electronics. Sometimes it goes wrong and the computer needs a 'brain transplant'.*

of storage have one thing in common: the data is coded as a series of noughts and ones. Much data in computers is stored on magnetic discs and tapes as a series of very small regions with north or south polarity, like the North Pole and South Pole of a magnet. The data is 'written' onto the tape with a series of electrical pulses and is 'read' by detecting the polarity of the regions and producing electrical pulses from these. It is quite like a cassette tape storing music, but computer tape only has noughts and ones on it, whereas a music tape has lots of variations in its magnetization.

Left *Computers form part of an exciting new service from the Post Office in the UK. Called Viewdata, the system needs only a modified television screen and a telephone, and the customer can have access to all sorts of up-to-date information. In the Home Magazine section, for instance, people at home can find information on news and weather, sport, radio and TV programmes, going out, holidays and tourism, travel and transport, hobbies and pastimes, jokes, quizzes and games.*

Left *Computers are used in space research. Here two physicists in America test a computer-controlled telescope. The instrument is used to search for supernovae — exploding stars millions and millions of miles away.*

Below *Another novel use for computers is in controlling the complicated lighting system in the new National Theatre in London.*

Help for hospitals

Mary Smithson felt rather nervous as she and her mother walked through the hospital entrance and over to the desk which was labelled 'New Patients'. Mary's mother handed the nurse behind the desk Mary's medical card. The nurse smiled and then turned to what looked like a typewriter keyboard and typed in Mary's name and medical card number.

Right *A computer terminal used in a hospital. These computers help hospital organization and make information ready for those who need it.*

Below *The nurse-receptionist is ready to deal with enquiries and visitors. In this case, the team are ready for emergencies because this is the casualty and emergency department.*

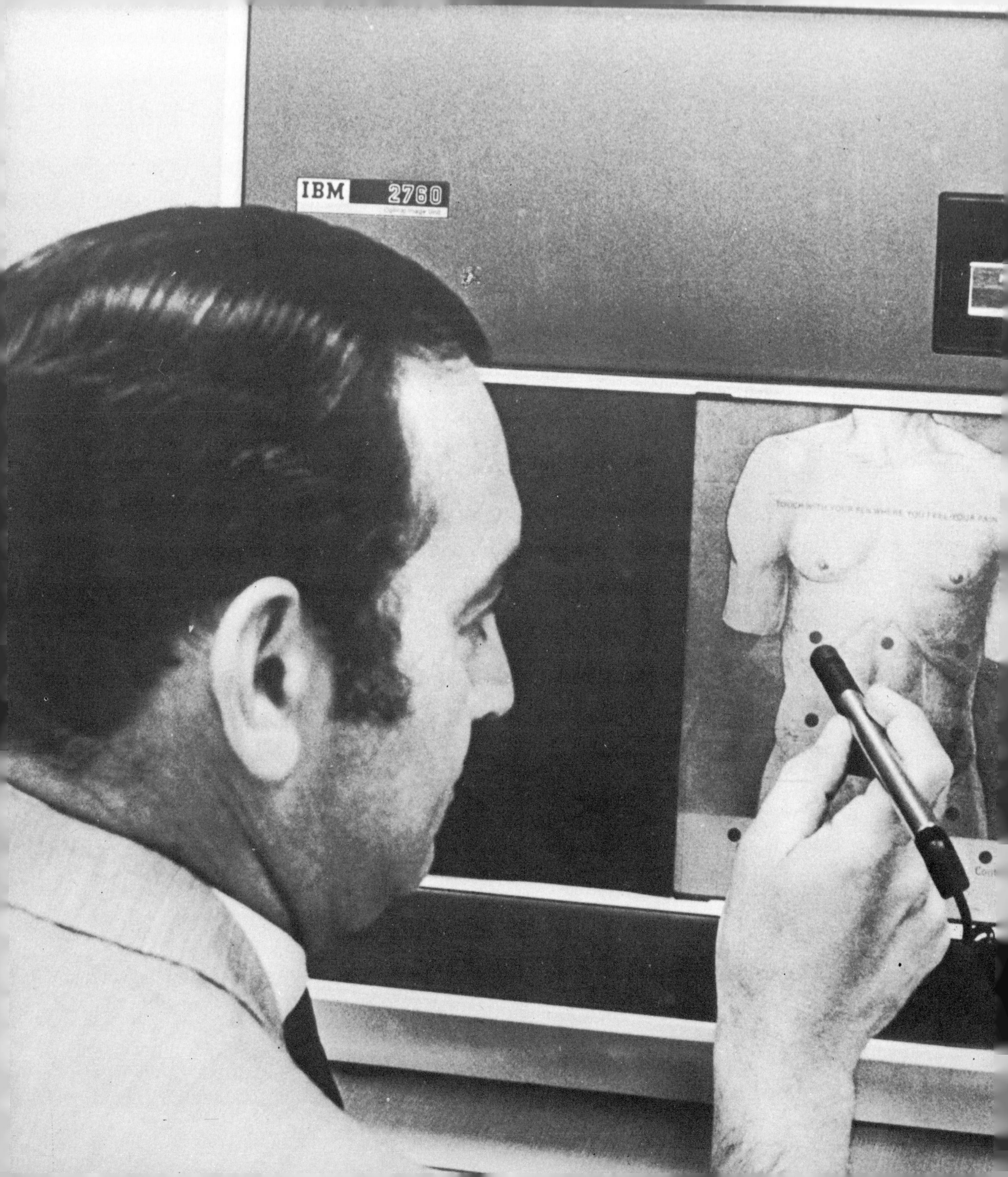
IBM 2760

"When you were here last, on June the 15th, you saw Dr Williams, didn't you?" she asked.

"Yes, that's right", said Mary's mother.

"Good," said the nurse. "I wanted to check that the computer has your record right and that I'd typed in your details correctly."

The television screen beside the keyboard had a lot of information on it and from this the nurse could see that Mary had come to have four teeth taken out. She could also see which ward Mary was to be in. She then took Mary and her mother there.

When the doctor came to see Mary the next morning he showed her a list, printed by the hospital computer, of the patients who were having operations that day. He told her that the computer worked out which patients went to which operating theatres and printed

A novel use for computers in medicine. The patient records his medical history by answering filmed questions. He answers the question "Where do you feel pain?" by indicating the exact spot with a light-pen. The computer processes the data ready for the doctor.

out lists for all the doctors and nurses so that they would know what was going on. When Mary heard that there were 1,500 patients in the hospital and twice that number who came in every day as out-patients, she realized how grateful the hospital staff were for the help the computer gave them.

"Just think," she said when her mother visited her that evening, "there are as many people in this hospital as there are in that new school I'm going to in September."

The ward sister who had come in with Mary's mother smiled. "But you are an easy patient," she said, "with no complications. The computer helps us most with really ill patients who may need certain medicines, perhaps different amounts each day for a few days and then something different or a special examination. You see, the doctor can decide on the treatment and record this on the computer, so that the nurses can be sure exactly what to do. The doctor's own timetable is also worked out so that each day he knows which patients he has to see. It makes sure he is not supposed to be in two places at

There are several security systems used with computers. Personal identity cards, punched with holes, tell computers who the user is and he is given only as much information as he is allowed to have. This security system also uses identity cards. If the man is allowed into the 'controlled area' the computer will send a signal to open the door.

This terminal at the patient's bedside gives the doctor instant case information, and will record nursing instructions. It can be moved around the ward.

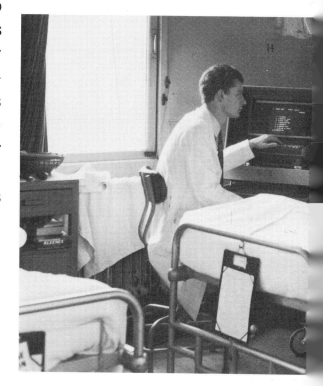

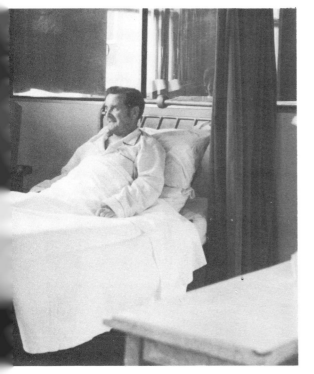

once, doing two different jobs."

Mary's mother was a little worried that people who were not supposed to have information about patients could just sit down at the typewriters connected to the computer (Sister said that they were called *'terminals'*) and find out what they wanted.

"Not a chance," smiled Sister, and showed them a small plastic card which she had to put into a slot on the terminal before she could use it. "That tells the computer who I am and the computer knows just how much information I am allowed to have. Nurses and doctors are given what information they need and no more."

When she was going home the next morning, Mary almost wanted to say Thank you to the computer, as well as to the doctors and nurses, for looking after her so well. But they would all carry on looking after her because she was given an appointment card, printed by the computer, for a check-up a few days later.

Right *The monitoring room in an Intensive Care Unit. The nurse can keep up-to-date with the progress of several patients at once.*

Below *Inside an Intensive Care Unit. In the foreground is a machine which helps keep the heart-beat regular after heart massage. You can see the control console on the right.*

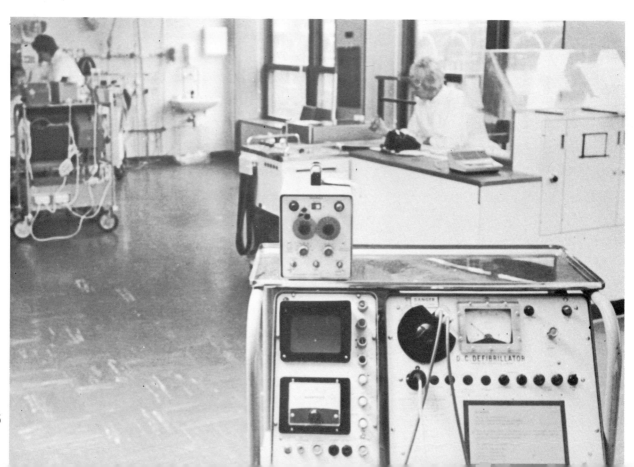

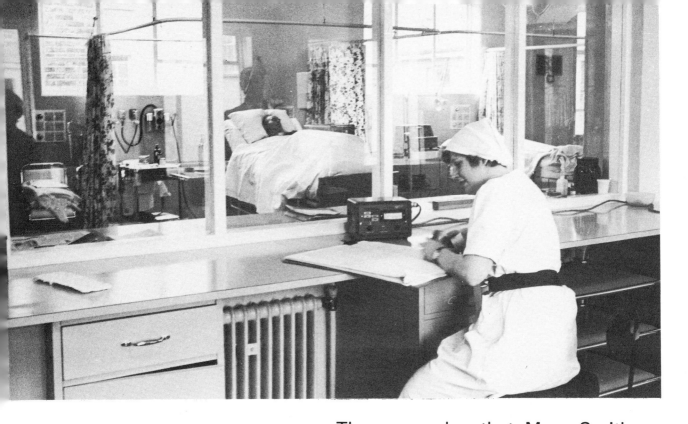

Below *The heart patient relaxes while the cardiograph shows the pattern of his heart-beats.*

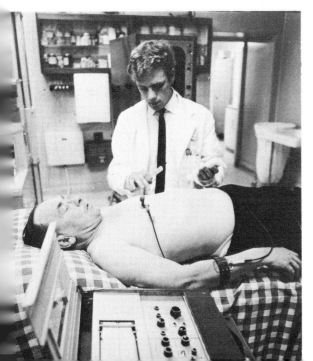

The same day that Mary Smithson had her teeth taken out, in the same hospital, a computer helped to save someone's life. Mr Hinton had been brought into hospital two days before Mary arrived. He was unconscious after a heart attack. He was very ill indeed, so the doctor put him in a bed in the Intensive Care Unit. Last year that would have meant that a nurse stayed with Mr Hinton every minute of the day and night, but now it was different. The nurses attached some wires and tubes to various parts of his body and the

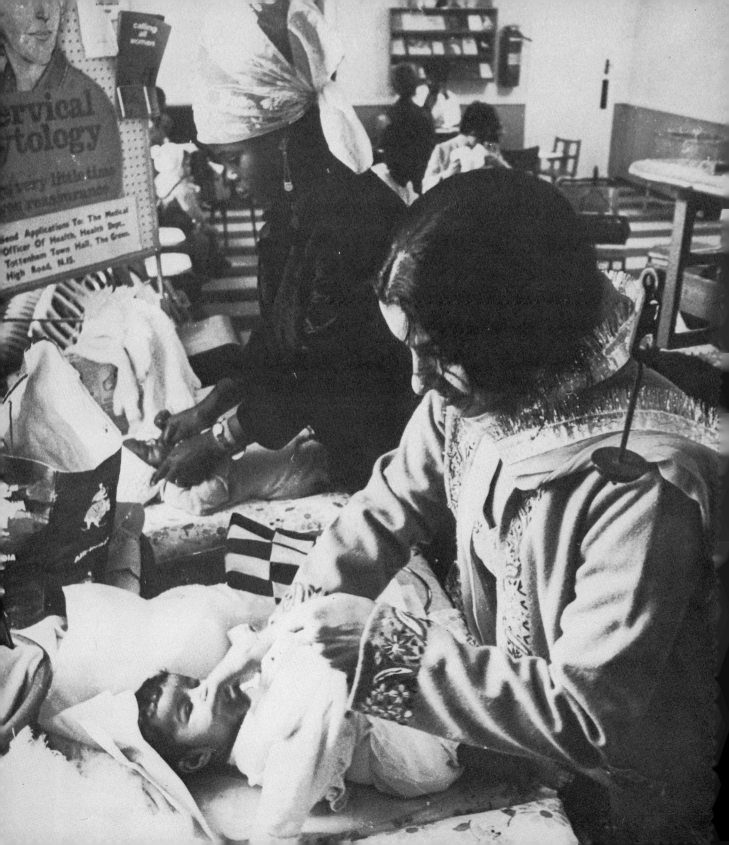

other ends were plugged into a small computer. This computer kept a check on Mr Hinton's pulse, his blood pressure, how fast he was breathing, and how well his heart was beating (using what doctors call an ECG — short for electrocardiograph). There were six other patients in the same unit, all six with just one nurse looking after them, and she was sitting in a control room. Each computer was connected to that control room.

That afternoon Mr Hinton's heart started beating in a strange way, and the computer immediately rang an alarm bell in the control room. The nurse there quickly called the doctor. Within seconds they were able to give Mr Hinton the attention he needed and without which he would have died.

Instant airline information

Have you ever thought how complicated it must be for an airline to keep track of all the seat bookings it gets? In the course of a year more than seven million people travel with a large international airline. On one flight this morning from London to New York, in three seats next to each other, there could be a businessman who booked his seat at three o'clock yesterday, an American flying round the world who booked his seat in New York four months ago, and a scientist who booked her seat in Glasgow three weeks ago.

The job of the people in airline offices is made much easier now that they have the help of computers. When the businessman booked his seat, almost

Right *BOAC 707 over Alaska. A busy
modern airline relies on computers
for seat bookings, cabin staff information,
air control and cargo handling.*

at the last minute, he went into the airline office and asked it there was any hope of a seat on one of today's planes to New York. The girl behind the counter used her terminal to type in 'London — New York' and today's date. Within five seconds a television screen

Passengers check in for their flight at Heathrow airport, London. On a busy summer day about a thousand flights leave Heathrow, so the computer's help is needed with timetables, baggage, passenger lists, and many more tasks.

Below *A terminal in the airline office at Victoria. Offices all over the country are linked to the same computer, and can give details of empty seats on all flights.*

above the terminal showed her the details of three flights to New York which had empty seats. The business-man chose the flight leaving at 10.30 and asked if the airline could book him into a hotel. The girl typed some more on the keyboard of the *video terminal*

and told the man that his seat was booked, ticket number JAX 30724; his seat number would be G7 and there was a room booked for him in the Bronsdon Hotel in New York. All of this was shown on the video screen in front of her. Two minutes later she handed the man his ticket, which had just been printed out on another terminal also linked directly to the computer.

There are many airline offices, all with terminals linked to the computer, and many of those terminals could be in use at the same time. This way of using a computer is called *'time - sharing'*. It means that the seat booked by the businessman that afternoon could well have been cancelled in Man-

Below *With their tickets and passports ready, these passengers check in for their flight. From now on their journey is under the care of computers as well as people.*

chester only five minutes earlier. Without the computer this would not have been known. Computers certainly speed up some jobs.

The same computer printed out a
complete list of all the passengers on
the same 10.30 London-to-New York
flight for the cabin stewardess to use.
The list told her how many of the

Below *The board gives information kept
up-to-the-minute by computer.*

Flight	Destination		Time
BA 561	BOSTON - NEW YORK		10.0
PA 805	TRINIDAD	BERMUDA-ANTIGUA BARBADOS	10.2
EC 725	NAIROBI-FRANKFURT		11.4
AI 104	PARIS-FRANKFURT-KUWAIT-BOMBAY-MADRAS-SINGAPORE-DJAKARTA		12.

DEPARTURE

passengers needed special meals, how many babies were on the flight, and that the gentleman in seat number H3 was an invalid who would need special help on the journey. There were also lists for

Left *The needs of the galley are printed by computer.*

Left *An operator in BOAC's vast cargo storage area feeds the computer information on where cargo is stored. Another operator can then find it easily.*

Below *Inside a warehouse for storing cargo at Heathrow. The computer helps with cargo handling and with clearance through customs.*

the pilot and co-pilot, telling them which hotel they would stay at in New York and that the next day they would be flying a Boeing 747 to Hawaii, take-off at 08:00 local time. The list of supplies for the galley, the aircraft kitchen, was also printed by the computer, to help the cabin staff.

The computer is a very large one, costing over two million pounds. It is helped by a number of smaller computers spread around the country; each costs about half a million pounds. It costs a lot to keep all these computers and the hundreds of terminals in touch with each other, but the airline saves money because better use is made of the aircraft and crews. It wastes money to run a flight half-empty.

Controlling air traffic is essential for safety. Air traffic controllers talk over the radio to the pilots, telling them when it is safe to take off and land. Other controllers watch the planes on radar screens.

The computer tells the cabin staff in
advance about passengers who will need
special help. Passengers in wheelchairs,
or who can only move with difficulty,
will receive special attention.

Computers catch criminals

At 07.10 on Thursday, 27th June, Police Officer Kennedy, who had just come on duty in his patrol car with Police Officer Bates, saw the front door of Edwards the jeweller's shop slightly open. P.C. Kennedy stopped the car and his partner went to investigate. Two minutes later he was back and sending a radio message to the local police station.

Portable telephone equipment is now more popular than computer terminals in police cars. The set can be locked in position in the car or carried about by the officer.

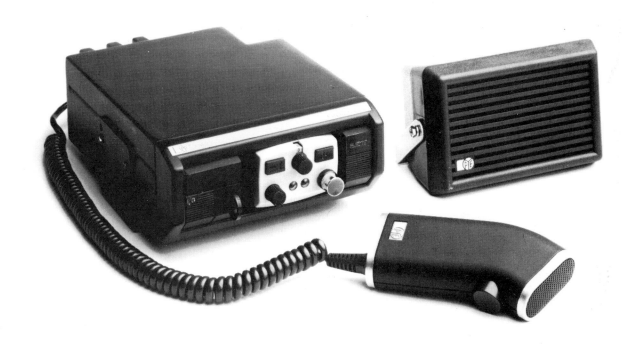

"Break-in at Edwards the jeweller's. Front entry, some damage, goods obviously missing. Awaiting instructions."

At the police station Sergeant Harris groaned. "That's the third jeweller's in two nights. When we have the details send them through to the area computer."

At the same time, ten miles away in another police station, Colonel Greystoke was angrily reporting the theft of his car. The station sergeant took down all the details — make, colour, registration, engine and chassis numbers. He

Computer terminals like these make police record work much easier. Data can be put into the system at the same time as other work is being processed. This does away with the need for computer cards or punched tape. Up to eight stations can be linked to the system.

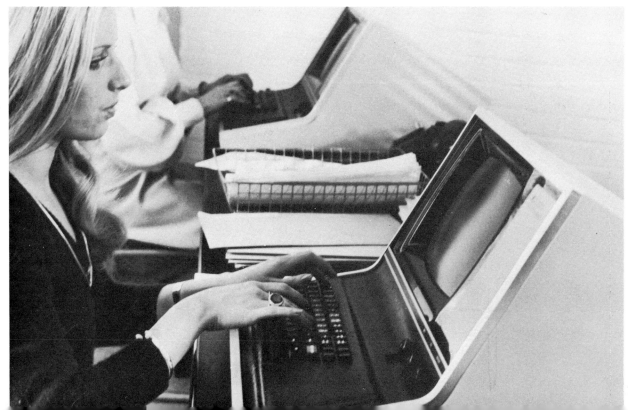

passed the piece of paper over to a young constable.

"Here you are, lad; another bit of data for the stolen vehicles file. Thank you, Colonel Greystoke. The infor-

Magnetic tape stores enormous amounts of information, especially useful for police records for which 'immediate access' is not required.

mation is being sent through to vehicle registration headquarters. Every county will know about it in half an hour's time. I'm sure that we shall soon have the car back for you, sir.''

By 08.30 Mr Edwards, the jeweller, had given the police a full description of the stolen property and already the local computer was searching its *data bank,* comparing the methods used in the break-in with the methods of known local criminals. At 08.53 the terminal in the police station typed out the names

Some police cars have these electronic 'touch maps'. They are mounted on the dashboard with a keyboard coding system. Routine messages are sent in code, and there is a red 'panic button' for use in an emergency.

of seven known criminals who worked in the way used at Mr Edwards' store. The information was interesting. Three of the criminals specialized in jewellery shops. Two of them had worked together before, and they had been released from jail only seven days earlier. The police moved fast, but neither of the men were at home when the police called.

Police cars speed on their way to make an arrest. Police efficiency is greatly helped by the computer-controlled information systems.

This is the Computer Terminal Bureau in New Scotland Yard. The terminals are linked with the Police National computer and can supply any officer with details of motor vehicles which have been reported as stolen, abandoned or suspected of being used in a crime.

At 10.15 P.C. Graham on foot-patrol reported a dark-green Jaguar, number AFC 10, parked behind a disused warehouse.

"I haven't seen a car there for a while," he said. "It's pretty unusual."

Sergeant Harris ran his finger down the list of last night's stolen cars, which had been printed out on the station terminal an hour and a half earlier.

A fingerprint expert dusts a stolen car to find fingerprints. Police records have details of over 2½ million fingerprints, taken from all convicted criminals in the UK.

Below In the Fingerprint Department the suspect's prints are compared with those on file. It takes the experts only a few minutes to say if the two prints match— and of course every person's fingerprints are unique.

"OK, Graham," he smiled. "You can telephone the police station that reported the missing Jaguar and tell them it's in one piece. This stolen vehicle file on the computer has certainly done a fine job today."

The Sergeant looked thoughtful. The warehouse where the car had been found was only a few hundred yards away from the house of one of the two men they had wanted to see about the break-in at the jeweller's. Could there be any connection?

The police were lucky. One of the two men had been careless and had left a set of fingerprints on the cigar lighter in

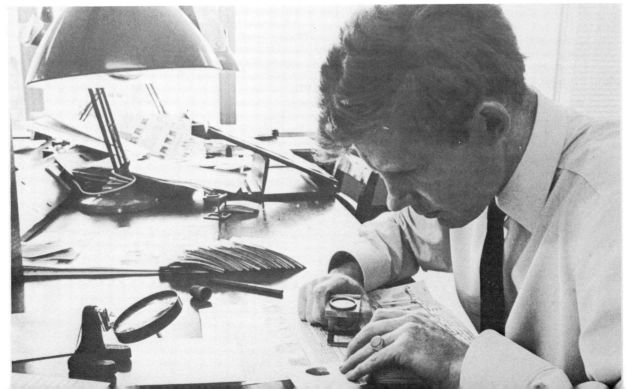

49

Colonel Greystoke's Jaguar. After some careful and clever questioning of the two suspects, charges were brought. Both men were soon back in jail, for a longer spell this time.

Computers do not help to solve every crime as neatly as these two, but they make the job of the police much easier by giving them information quickly when it is needed.

Computers in use in Scotland Yard. These operators are processing a new set of prints to go in the National Fingerprint Collection.

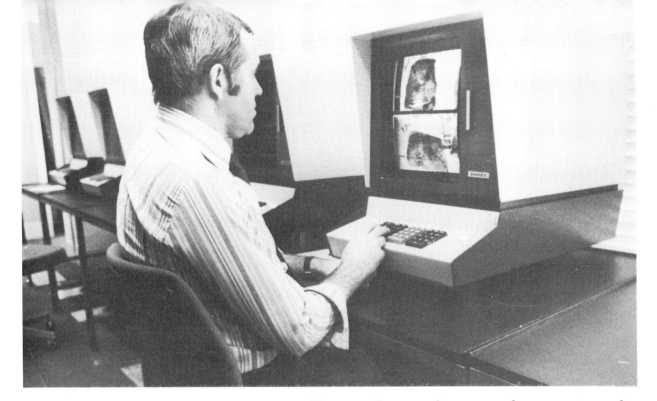

A Fingerprint Officer can then retrieve the processed prints and compare them with others. The prints are stored on magnetic tape and can be recalled through the central computer to video terminals.

The police make use of computers in many other ways. By getting information on vehicle and drivers' licences they find people who drive dangerously. Information on criminals from all around the world is available to the police forces in many countries through the police international organization, Interpol, and this is found quickly with the help of computers. Without information from computer files the police would not be able to catch many of the well-organized gangs of criminals who attempt great robberies and other crimes.

Stocking the supermarket

The last time you were in your local supermarket, did you notice labels on the shelves which seemed to be made of just vertical straight lines? They probably told you nothing at all!

When the manager of the supermarket wants to order some more soap, spaghetti, coffee, or any of the hundreds of things he sells, these curious labels make the job easier. One of the assistants carries a very special box with some push-buttons on it and a tube, about eight or ten centimetres (3½in) long, attached by a wire to the box. The tube is called a *light-pen,* not because it is not heavy, but because it is a way of recording light and dark marks. The assistant moves the end of the light-pen across the lines on the shelf label, and all the details of the goods are recorded on a magnetic tape inside the box. It works rather like a tape recorder, and the magnetic tape is similar to the tape used in a tape

In a busy branch of a supermarket chain, an assistant records what goods are needed for the next day. She carries a special box and light-pen, and runs the pen across labels on each shelf. The computer can tell which goods are on the shelf by the pattern of black lines on the label – see if you can find these labels on your supermarket shelves.

recorder but wider. The assistant then uses the push-buttons on the box to record, also on the magnetic tape, the number of packets the shop wants to order. When this has been done for all the food the shop wants to order, the magnetic tape is put into a special terminal. All the data on the tape is then sent to the computer belonging to the chain of supermarkets.

When the orders have been collected from all the supermarkets in a large area of the country, the computer works out totals of all the foods needed. It also works out the best way of loading the delivery vehicles which take orders to the supermarkets, so that no time or fuel is wasted. From the computer, details of the orders and the deliveries are sent to delivery depots. Special telephone lines connect the terminals to the depots. This way the supermarkets get their food quickly, when they need it, and while it is fresh. Customers are kept happy and find as few gaps as possible on the super-market shelves.

The job the computer is doing is

In the computer department of the supermarket chain, the orders received from the branches are processed, and sent in turn to the warehouse.

called *data processing.* The computer takes the data (the orders from the supermarkets) and it processes the data — that is, it produces new data (in this case, delivery lists).

Some shops, especially clothes shops interested in how fashions are changing, use a different method of getting data to their computer. Perhaps when you buy a jersey the sales assistant may take the sales ticket attached to the jersey, give half to you and keep half for the shop. If the sales ticket is a 'Kimball Tag' it will have holes punched in it. This is a special kind of *punched card,* used in a popular method of putting data into a computer. The tag will have the size, colour, price and reference number of the jersey printed on it, and the pattern of the holes will allow the computer to read the same information. At the end of the day, all the tags from all the shop's depart-

The warehouse receives order lists, and can quickly dispatch the goods each branch needs. The computer will also work out the most economical way of delivering the goods, so that they arrive fresh and when they are needed.

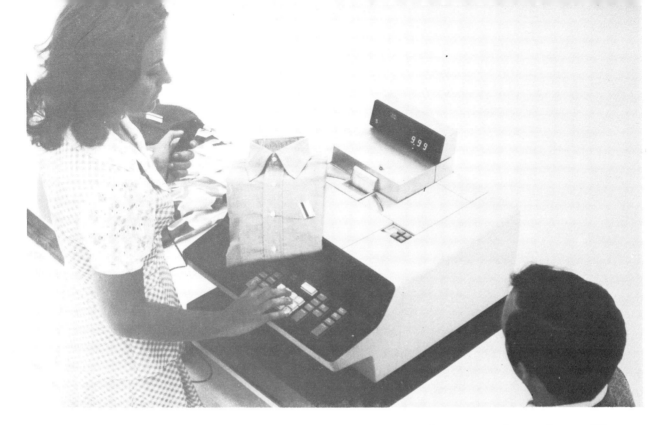

Above *This clothes shop uses a point-of-sale' device; the salesgirl passes a magnetic wand reader over the coded card on the garment.*

ments are put into *card readers*. These read the holes on the cards and put the data into the computer, perhaps directly, perhaps using telephone lines again.

The computer uses the data to print out reports for each manager, telling them which fashions are selling well, how much money has been made by each shop, when clothes need to be moved from the warehouse to the shops, and much more that a manager needs to know to help run the business well.

Left *The terminal at the point-of-sale with the magnetic wand reader. This is a quick way of recording what the shop is selling; in this case, it is a cardigan.*

Sorting out the traffic

How can a traffic warden or policeman, controlling the traffic in Piccadilly Circus, London, know how busy the traffic is half a mile away in Oxford Street? There is no easy way for him to know and he cannot really hope to arrange the movement of cars and buses round Piccadilly Circus so as to help the traffic keep moving in other parts of London.

A police officer on point duty in the busy London traffic. Police and traffic wardens were once needed at junctions when traffic-lights broke down.

Below A typical London traffic jam before the introduction of computerized traffic-lights.

Inside the Metropolitan Police Traffic Control Centre, in New Scotland Yard.

Traffic-lights used to change their signals automatically after a fixed time had passed. Many still do that, but in some cities a large computer at police headquarters does the job. To find out where the traffic is, hundreds of wires have been buried in the surface of the streets and each wire, or detector, as it is called, sends electrical signals to the computer whenever a vehicle passes over it. So many of these electrical signals arrive back at the computer every second that *two* computers are needed. A 'message' computer organizes the signals coming in, and a 'control' computer works out the best way to arrange the workings of the traffic-lights. The aim is to keep the number of

delays as few as possible. It would take a human a long time to work out this problem, but the computer can do the difficult calculations much faster. Before a human had got very far with the calculation, the numbers of cars in

Maps of the area, showing the busy junctions, help the officer who will be in control of the traffic-lights if the computer breaks down.

Inside the Traffic Control Radio Room where officers can keep watch on traffic movements.

the streets would have changed and he or she would have to start again.

In the control room at police headquarters there are special screens which show the operators street maps, just how much traffic is in each street,

what signal each traffic-light is showing and how much time each light is spending on red or green. If the system breaks down (which does not happen often) there are spare computers to take over. If there is some other kind of emergency the operators have control *consoles* so that they can take control of any set of traffic-lights. As well as all this, there are television screens which show pictures from television cameras placed high above the streets and corners which get especially busy. These cameras, usually perched on the top of office blocks or stores can be adjusted by signals from the operators in the control room.

Computers help the police with traffic problems in another way. This screen can show the average speed at which a car is moving, and so help the officers tell if anyone is breaking the speed limits.

Above *Directing the traffic is now a rare task, thanks to the computers. Patrolling police have more time to help people in the city.*

Over the page *The remote-controlled camera surveys the scene from a high view-point in London.*

The computer keeps a record of the traffic patterns and the traffic-light settings, so that experts can look at them again later to see if any improvements can be made. Now, a journey which used to take half an hour takes only twenty-five minutes. There are fewer accidents now that computers control the lights.

Making roads and bridges

There are many stages in any modern engineering project. Whether it is a road, a bridge, a motor-car or a computer there are at least three stages where computers can help the engineers — in the planning, in the design and in the construction itself.

Right *New techniques in bridge-building are helped at the design stage by using computers.*

Below *Building a new motorway. Computers help cost the operation, and work out the best route.*

When a new motorway is to be built, there are very many alternative routes that it may take. The choice will be affected by the position of existing roads, houses, factories, farms and so on. The choice will also be affected by the cost of moving earth to produce a level road and the cost of building bridges and junctions. The opinion of local people will influence the decision and the total cost of each alternative will have to be worked out carefully. Before it can work out the cost, the computer needs to know the layout of the land, the kind of rocks under the surface, the positions of rivers, roads and drains, and many other pieces of local information. The computer program can then calculate the costs of the various alternatives and so help in the planning of the new motorway.

Right *The architect gives the computer the specific requirements, and it produces a suitable design. The architect can alter this design by marking changes with a light-pen. The computer then makes these alterations.*

Far Right *The computer produces calculations about a new bridge, and the surveyors use the figures to check that all is going well with the construction.*

An engineer designing a bridge is helped by being able to see quickly how his or her ideas will turn out when seen from different directions. The computer will work out how thick the supports and sections of the arch have to be so that the bridge will be strong enough. It will then produce a drawing for the engineer. This drawing is often

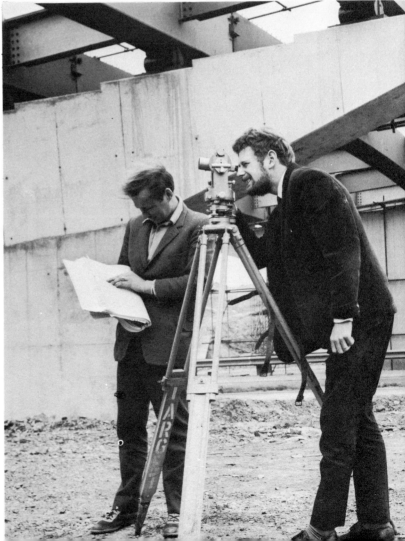

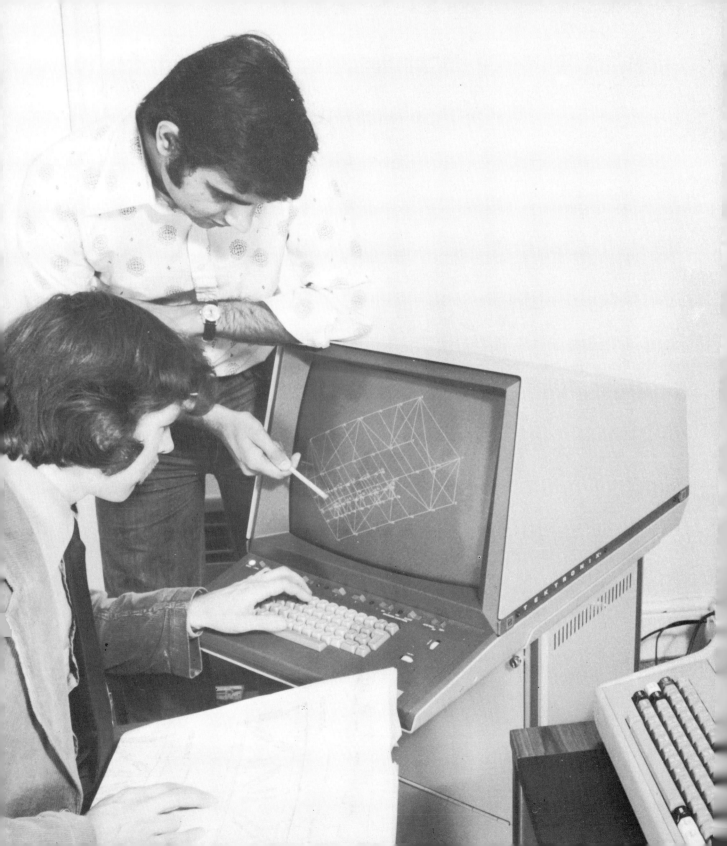

Left *The computer can check whether the engineer's design is strong enough, as well as making sure that it will not be too expensive to carry out. Here the engineer checks his drawing against the computer's, and types in any alterations.*

produced on a video terminal and the engineer is able to ask for a view of the bridge from any angle. The designer may then wish to make a number of changes by actually drawing these changes with a light-pen on the screen or by typing in new sizes and angles on the keyboard. The computer will then redraw the pictures in a matter of seconds and also check that the strength and cost of the bridge are within the limits set by the construction company. The drawing and calculations for each change would take many days if they were done by the engineer.

Once a good design has been found,

Right *This civil engineer makes alterations to the computer's design with a light-pen. She will be able to see the changes made immediately. This function of computers saves weeks of work for people.*

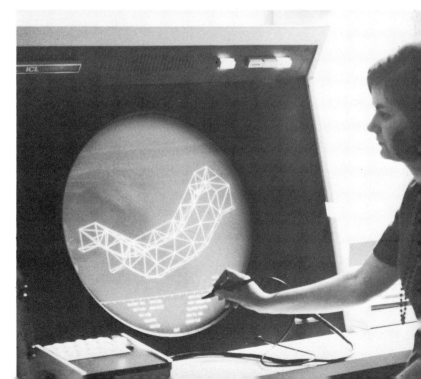

the computer will be able to produce a detailed drawing to scale on paper by controlling a huge drawing machine called a *plotter*. It will also list all the materials needed and may order these from a supplier so that they arrive for the workmen at the right time.

In some cases the computer may even play a part in the actual construction of the parts. Computers are used to control machines which cut and drill parts for cars, washing machines, tractors and many other everyday objects. The piece of metal to be cut or

Right *Steel girders are drilled in an engineering plant. The drilling is all controlled by computer.*

Below *This I-shaped girder is being drilled with holes. The computer moves the girder into the right place and makes sure that the holes are the right size. The planning, design, costing and even the production of parts for roads and bridges is helped by computer. Large civil engineering projects may cost millions of pounds, and computers can avoid waste, and dangerous errors.*

drilled is put on a table which can be moved in all three directions by electric motors. The drills and cutting tools are normally kept in one place and the piece of metal moved round them. The details of the shape to be cut are fed in to the computer and the computer then calculates all the electrical pulses, in the correct order for controlling the drilling and cutting machines. These pulses are then recorded on magnetic tape, or perhaps on *paper tape*, which is about two centimetres wide and punched with holes. The tape is then passed through the control unit of the drilling or cutting machine which then works on its own until the piece of metal is the correct shape and size.

Computers already help to make some parts of computers. Very skilled men and women design the computer circuits, but then a computer can work out the best way of wiring the design, and can produce punched paper tape to

Here you can see the actual computer controls which govern the making of machine tools.

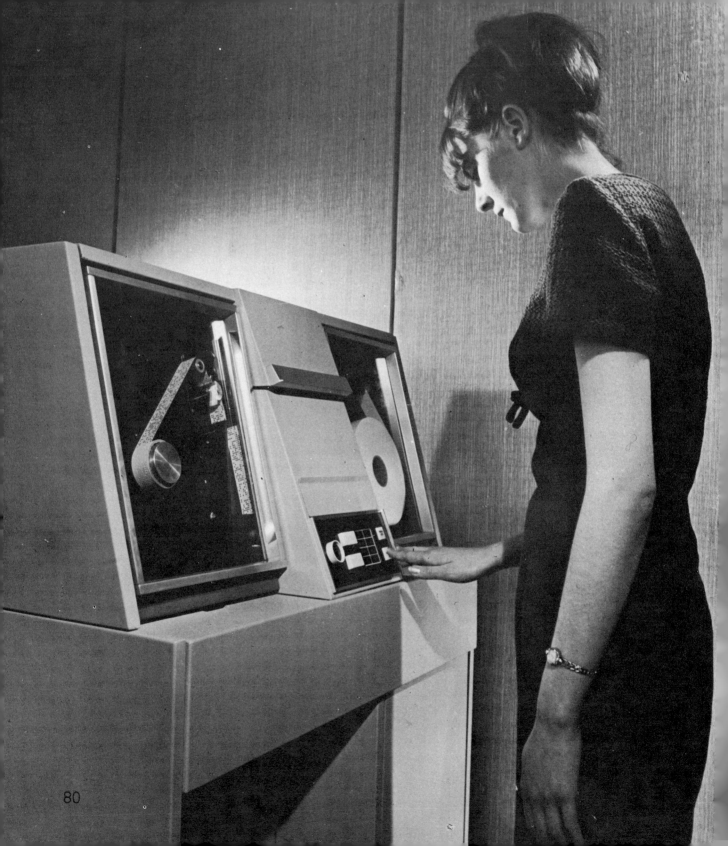

Above *This machine 'reads' the information on paper tape which then falls into the basket for easy disposal.*

Left *Here the paper tape is being punched with holes. The machine can punch 150 characters in a second.*

control the wiring machine. Computers can be used to test those parts of computers which store information, and find out if any one of the thousands of parts is not working properly.

The completed project—a motorway and bridge combined. All along the way, the project has been helped by the use of computers.

Finding out More

You might ask one of your teachers to arrange for your class to visit a computer. There are many firms with their own computers, or if you live in a large city you may be near to the computer for a chain of supermarkets or a department store.

Books to read

Carey D, *How it Works: The Computer* (Ladybird, 1971)
Clark J O E, *Computers at Work* (Hamlyn, 1969)
Fairlie T H, Neil C M, & Flockhart H S, *Computers in Action* (Oliver and Boyd, 1972)
Hollingdale S H & Tootill G C, *Electronic Computers* (Pelican, 1970)
London K, *Introduction to Computers* (Faber & Faber, 1974)
Scottish Computers in Schools Project, *The Computer: Yours Obediently II: Man Uses the Computer* (Chambers, 1972)

Glossary

ANALYST   A person who analyses the whole task and decides how much should be done by computer and how it should be done.

CARD READER   A machine which detects holes in a punched card and sends the information contained in them to the computer.

CONSOLE   Part of a computer used by an operator, containing a keyboard, switches and panels showing what the computer is doing.

DATA   Information, facts and figures.

DATA BANK   A collection or store of information.

DATA PROCESSING   The rearrangement of data and calculations using data.

LIGHT-PEN   A tool which is sensitive to light, often used in connection with a video terminal.

LINE PRINTER   A printing unit connected to a computer.

MAGNETIC TAPE   Tape coated with magnetizable material, used for storing information.

MAGNETIC DISC   Similar to tape but shaped like a gramophone record; used for storing information which is needed quickly.

OPERATOR   A person who runs the computer, feeding in information and sending the results back to the programmer or analyst.

PAPER TAPE   Tape carrying information in the form of punched holes, used for putting information into a computer.

PLOTTER   A machine used for drawing plans and

diagrams.

PROGRAM   A set of instructions to enable a computer to carry out a job.

PROGRAMMER   A person who writes a program.

PUNCHED CARD   A card carrying information in the form of punched holes.

TERMINAL   A machine used for sending information to a computer and receiving information from a computer.

TIME-SHARING   A number of people using one computer at the same time; sometimes called multi-access.

VIDEO TERMINAL   A terminal with a television screen.

Index

Picture Credits

The authors and publishers wish to thank those who kindly gave their permission for copyright pictures to appear on the following pages: Barclays Bank, 8(right); BOAC, 10, 14, 30-31; British Airports, 32, 40; British Airways, 8-9, 33, 34, 35, 41; Camera Press, 28, 29; Central Office of Information for Crown Copyright pictures, 26, 27(below), 65; Cement & Concrete Association, 71; Central Press, 50, 51; Commissioner of Police at New Scotland Yard, 46, 47, 48, 61, 62, 64, 66, 67; Elliot Bros (London) Ltd, 9; Ford, 16; GEC/Elliot Automatic, 36-37(top); IBM, 12, 12-13, 22-23, 25, 44, 58, 59, 72-73; ICL, 17, 38, 43, 73, 76, 77, 80, 81; Keystone Press, 68-69; John Laing & Son Ltd, 70; Oracle/ITCA, 18(below); Pan American World Airways, 36-37(top); Post Office, 18(top); J. Sainsbury Ltd, 53, 54, 56-57; *The Times*, 27(top). All other pictures are the property of the Wayland Picture Library.